ON THE UNDERGRO[UND]
Set 2
The Strange and the Exotic

I Dreams

Text
ROBERT HERRICK
1591-1674

Music
THEA MUSGRAVE
(1994)

Misterioso ♩= 52

SOPRANO
pp
Here ___ we ___ are all, ___ by

ALTO
pp
Here ___ by ___

TENOR
pp
Here, here we are all, ___

BASS

Misterioso ♩= 52

PIANO
(for rehearsal
only)

5

day; ___ by night, ___ by night we are

p
day; ___ by night, ___

by ___ day; ___ by night ___ we are

By night ___ we are hurled ___ by

5

Commissioned by Ithaca College School of Music.
First performance October 29th, 1994. *Duration: c. 5 minutes.*

COMPOSER'S NOTE

There is one unexpected pleasure taking the London Underground (and, more recently, also New York City subway): one's eye may alight on a poem placed amongst the pervasive and numbing advertisements, and, for a moment, the imagination takes wing.

The three poems selected for this work are all to be found in *100 Poems on the Underground*. The first, by Robert Herrick describes the dream world, the setting where the "wondrous sights" of the anonymous 17th century poem can be found. Fortunately the subway piranhas of Edwin Morgan's contemporary poem exist only in the imagination. However, this poem, commissioned for the inauguration of Glasgow's refurbished underground, so alarmed the transport executive that it was never used!

T.M.

[*circa 45"*]

II I Saw A Peacock With A Fiery Tail

Text
Anonymous
17th Century

Music
THEA MUSGRAVE

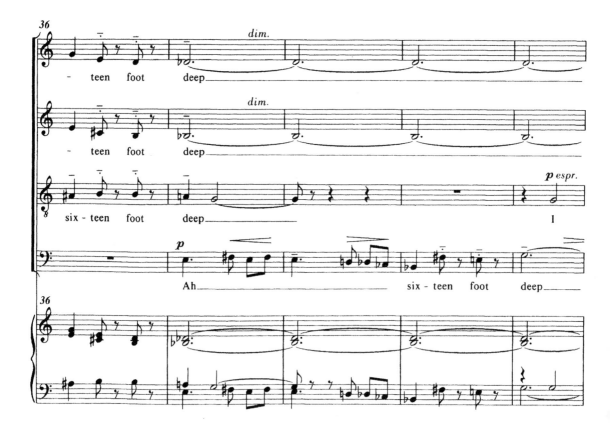

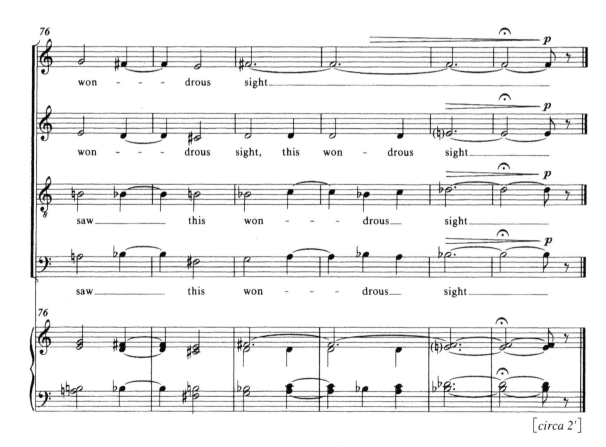

[*circa 2'*]

III The Subway Piranhas*

Text
EDWIN MORGAN
[b. 1920]

Music
THEA MUSGRAVE

* This poem, commissioned for the inauguration of Glasgow's refurbished underground, so alarmed the transport
executive that it was never used.

seat is a tank of pi-ra-nha fish which have

not been fed for quite some time.

La la la la la la la la la la la la la la la la

la la la la la la la la la

la___ The fish be - come a - gi-ta - ted by the

la___ The fish be - come a - gi-ta - ted by the

The fish be - come a - gi-ta - ted by the

The fish be - come a - gi-ta - ted by the

in me-di-cal schools

la la la la la la la la la la la la la la la la la la

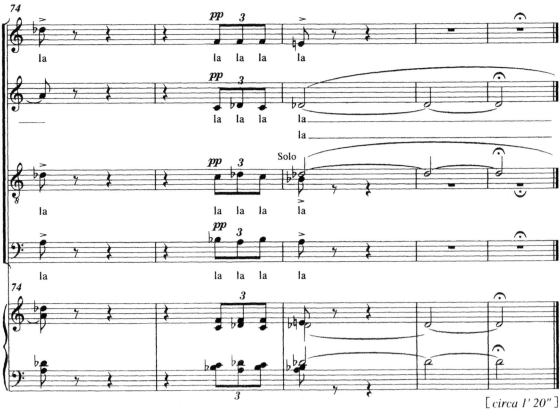

[*circa 1' 20"*]

IV Dreams [reprise]

[*circa* 50"]

Published by Novello Publishing Limited
Music setting by Stave Origination
Printed in Great Britain